THE AMAZING ADVENTURES

OF

BERTIE THE BORDER TERRIER

A W M PRIESTLEY

for Lyndia - July 15th 2013

Completely Novel 2013

~

ISBN : 9781849144049

~

printers : CPI

~

dtp & layout : alchemy design

THE BORDER TERRIER

Head like an otter.
Moderately broad
skull with short
strong muzzle.
Black nose preferred.
Eyes dark with
keen expression.

Ears. Small V-shaped.
Moderate thickness
dropping forward
close to cheek

Tail.
Moderately short,
fairly thick at base
then tapering. Set
high. Not curled over
back. Carried gaily.

Forequarters.
Forelegs straight, not
too much bone.

Hindquarters.
Racy, loin strong.

Coat.
Harsh and dense with
close thick undercoat.
Skin must be thick.

Feet.
Small with thick pads.

Body.
Deep and narrow,
ribs carried
well back.
Not oversprung.

Colour:-
Red.
Wheaten.
Grizzle and tan.
Blue and tan.

Weight and Size. Dogs.   13 - 15½ lbs.
                 Bitches.   11½ - 14 lbs.

illustration from the Official Breed Standard

My thanks to Grian who has kindly taken much time and care to draw such imaginative illustrations which do so much to help this book come alive. Grian has owned several champion whippets and she has specialised in drawing, painting and sculpting this breed. She had three bronze whippet models exhibited at the Paris Salon which were later sold through the Sladmore gallery in London's Mayfair. Two of her other bronze models were bought by an Egyptian collector when they were exhibited on the Cote d'Azur. Grian lives in France, in a beautiful corner of the Normandy countryside.

CONTENTS

BURLINGTON BERTIE

I'm Burlington Bertie, I rise at ten-thirty

And reach Kempton Park around three.

I stand by the rail when a horse is for sale,

And you ought to see Wooton watch me.

I lean on some awning while Lord Derby's yawning,

Then he bids two thousand and I bid "Good Morning".

I'm Bert, Bert, I'd buy one, a Cert,

But where would I keep it you know?

I can't let my man see me in bed with a gee-gee.

I'm Burlington Bertie from Bow!

A verse from Burlington Bertie a music hall song
Composed by Harry B Norris in 1900
and sung by Vesta Tilley.

For my friend Freddie

INTRODUCTION

B ertie is an Essex boy. He is a red grizzle Border Terrier with bright, brown eyes, floppy ears and a rough coat. He was born at Fobbing Acres near Basildon. He was a mistake. He was meant to be a cross between a Border and a Jack Russell but his father got at the breeder's elderly Border bitch. So out he popped, a pure--bred Border Terrier.

When he is only four months old Bertie finds himself in the back of a car in the bowels of a ferry sailing to Calais. He has his own passport showing his photo stamped with the required vaccinations, including rabies.

His adventures begin when he arrives in the region of Aquitaine, a corner of France known as 'Little England' and the department the English ex-pats call 'Dordogneshire'. Eight hundred years ago, back in the 12th century, Aquitaine was ruled from Bordeaux by the English King, Henry II who married Queen Eleanor of Aquitaine*.

Like our late King Henry himself no doubt, Bertie struts his stuff hunting rabbits and deer among the vines and adjoining woodland.

After being christened by burning mice falling from a nest in a chimney he becomes a champion mouse catcher. He comes first in his class at the Bordeaux International Dog show but is disqualified for only having one testicle.

He sees off unfriendly French rivals - hunting dogs like Teckels, Basset Hounds and Mastiffs called Dogue de Bordeaux*. His best friend is a French terrier bitch called Vicky. He meets Chinese wine merchants buying up thousands of Bordeaux Grands Crus in St. Emilion. In a local bar he comforts a half blind former British soldier - an Iraq war veteran suffering from post traumatic stress.

On a visit to the Camargue he jumps into a bullring where he proceeds to bait a fierce young bull who tosses him in the air. Luckily he escapes being gored to death by the bull's horns.

Later he finds himself on the tiny Channel Island of Alderney. He comes first in the agility class at the Alderney dog show. On his way back to England from France, he gets stuck in Spain with the wrong stamp in his passport.

Back in London, being an entire male, albeit with only one testicle, Bertie scraps with other entire dogs, large or small. He has a penchant for fluffy types like Pomeranians, Poodles and King Charles Spaniels whose fur he likes to grab in his teeth. He has no fear of larger dogs, such as Staffordshire Bull Terriers, from whom he often has to be prised apart.

Surprisingly, Bertie later comes under the calming influence of an urban fox. They become the best of friends when Bertie gets lost and the fox shows him the way home.

The following stories are seen through Bertie's eyes and told, in what I imagine to be, his own words.

4

Dogue de Bordeaux (Bordeaux Dog) was known in France as early as the 14th Century, particularly in south-west France in the Bordeaux region. That's why the city gave its name to this breed. It is similar to the English Mastiff, believed to pre-date the Bull Mastiff and the Bulldog. One theory is that the Dogue de Bordeaux originates from the Tibetan Mastiff.

A massive dog, powerfully built, the Dogue de Bordeaux is- thick set with heavy boned front legs and cat-like feet. Its average weight is 7 stone and it stands at about 3 feet in height. The Dogue de Bordeaux is said to have the largest head in the canine world. According to locals these unique dogs at one time used to carry in their mouths large cuts of meat from the old Capucine market in Bordeaux delivering them to regular clients. Another Dogue de Bordeaux owner warns other prospective owners that these dogs don't listen, and adds that they will decide what to do whenever they feel like it.

BERTIE
GOES TO
BORDEAUX

I was only four months old when my owners decided to take me with them to France. They took me to the vet in London and I was given an anti-rabies jab. Apparently I couldn't get infected by rabies in Britain but the virus still exists on the continent. If a dog with rabies bites someone, even if it's just an ankle, then that unfortunate person could easily die. It will be a slow and painful death. First he will become delirious, his or her hair will stand up, he will become aggressive wanting to bite people and he will have a manic fear of water.

The anti-rabies jab made me feel a bit low for a couple of days. Then I was given my own passport with a blue cover. My microchip number, my rabies inoculation and the date I was wormed were listed inside.

Then off we went to Dover in their car. They made an awful fuss filling the back seat with extra cushions and blankets for me to sleep on. They had even bought me a little portable radio broadcasting classical music to calm me for the crossing. When they told me I had to stay in the car after we drove onto the ferry I realised why. It was dark and rather scary down there on deck 5. I could hear the chugging of the boat's engines and the sea rushing by.

"How long was I going to have to stay in this horrible place ?" I asked myself.

Finally I managed to get to sleep.

I woke up to the noise of car engines revving up and the smell of exhaust fumes. Then my owners arrived and made more fuss of me.

"Good boy. Have some water. Have you had a good sleep? We will soon be on dry land when you can have walkies," they told me.

I must say I was pleased to see them but not so pleased to be shut in the car for ages. I ignored them to show my displeasure.

They told me we were in a place called France - a foreign country inhabited by people who didn't speak English. They spoke a different language called French. My parents warned me that they didn't really like us English humans and animals because we had beaten them in many wars over the centuries, and they didn't hunt foxes the same way we do in England.

My parents gave me a short history lesson. At Crécy our archers won a decisive battle in the Hundred Years War; in 1415 at Agincourt, Henry V and his archers slaughtered the French cavalry and men at-arms; four hundred years later, the Duke of Wellington beat Napoleon at Waterloo, and just a few years earlier Admiral Lord Nelson won a great victory at sea sinking the French fleet at The Battle of Trafalgar.

Us dogs were used to help our soldiers fight against the French. Henry VIII sent hundreds of war dogs to help Charles V of Spain to fight the French. They were reported to have acquitted themselves with great credit at the siege of Valencia.

I was heartened by these stories of our victories against the French. I am a terrier bred to hunt foxes and I had no intention of being intimidated by these strangers.

For two days we travelled through countryside and cities quite different to London. I was very tired when we at last arrived in an area of France known as the Lot-et-Garonne and a departement called Aquitaine. My owners had a little house on the edge of a small hamlet called Masquieres. We had to go up a drive and through a dairy farm to get to the house.

The next morning I saw a group of heifers in a field at the bottom of our lane. This would be fun, I thought. I dived under the fence and gave chase. This wasn't a good idea. They started bucking and kicking and one of them caught me off guard, landing a kick squarely on my head.

Dazed, I went home and had to lie down.

When I woke up I had a bit of a headache, but all my marbles seemed to be in place. My owners were distraught and thought I might have been at death's door. To celebrate my recovery they decided to enter me in the Bordeaux International Dog Show.

This was all because a judge at a country show in England - at Berkeley Castle in Gloucestershire - told my owners that I was one of the best looking Border Terriers she had seen. I think she was trying to console them for failing to get me entered in the puppy class. I was too young at the time - under three months old and to qualify I had to be three months or more.

Off we set for Bordeaux in the pouring rain at the crack of dawn. The dog show was in an enormous covered arena. There must have been nearly a thousand of my four-legged friends and their owners in this vast space, the size of three football pitches.

We found the Terrier ring where we met a German lady with five Border Terriers. She said she had been breeding and showing Border Terriers for many years. She told us what to do. I had to wait to be called by the judge. Then I would have to be led round the ring a few times. After a few circuits I would be placed on a table so the judge could have a closer inspection.

I remained on my best behaviour and strutted round the ring, my tail up and my best paw forward. The judge appeared suitably impressed. That was until I had to stand on his table for a closer inspection. I was upset to find the judge started examining my privates. Having squeezed one of my testicles he began groping around for the other one which was still in my stomach.

His examination finished abruptly; he told my owner to take me out of the ring. I had been disqualified, he said, because only one of my testicles had dropped. This was a great shame because I was the only male Border Terrier in the puppy class and it would have been a walkover. I would have come away with a lovely silver cup and a big red First-in-Class rosette.

If this had been England I would have won my class because the judges there don't disqualify puppies with only one testicle.

"Typical bloody French," I said

Would you believe it though? The judge was an Englishman.

BERTIE

AND

VICKY

Soon after appearing at the dog show in Bordeaux my owners sold their little house in the Lot-et-Garonne and bought a larger property in the Dordogne. It is surrounded by vineyards, woodland and fields of maize so I am able to seek out and chase the animals that live therein.

Our new house is, in fact, old and draughty. There are cracks in the floorboards with an abundance of mice running around beneath the floor across the earth foundations. The house has a tall, sloping "Périgourdine" roof under which there is a huge attic where other mice and the odd rat can be found. Outside in the courtyard I chase lizards and frogs that appear from under tiles and stones where they have been hiding from the sun or sleeping in the heat of the day.

Another distraction is our neighbour's mongrel bitch terrier called Vicky. She looks something like a cross between a Dachshund and a Poodle. She has thick, black, curly hair and a tail with a brush at the end of it like a Poodle's. She has a long body more like a Dachshund's.

She is very playful and very fast. She outruns me and she has enormous stamina. When we go for walks together she goes for miles and chases rabbits and deer. She has been teaching me how to hunt deer, hares, rabbits, coypu and foxes. Boy, does she shift across the fields but she always comes back to find us.

You might not know much about Coypu. Known as the river rat, they have large yellow incisor teeth which I know only too well. I was borrowing down one of their tunnels near a small lake when I came face to face with one. It bared its teeth but backed off after I sank my own sharp molars into its neck.

Every morning Vicky comes across from our neighbour's house which is just behind our own place. She pushes the back door open and jumps onto my owners bed and wakes me up. I like to have a lie-in after the humans are up and I hide underneath the covers but Vicky always finds me.

Our house has floorboards in every room so we chase each other up and down the length of the ground floor rooms, slipping and sliding on the polished floors. This irritates my owners enough to persuade one of them to take us for a walk through the vines and fields that adjoin our property.

Vicky belongs to Carla, the young Portuguese girlfriend of Stephan Prevot. They live with Stephan's mother, Marie Reine, in the house immediately behind our own. Carla works tending the vines and Stephan's mother works as a "prunier". One of her jobs is to extract the stones from thousands of ripe plums. She does this with a special tool, a bit like ones used for corking wine but it extracts rather than inserts.

Stephan is a carpenter, and while he was fixing the floor boards in our house he told us about his other job working as a part-time gamekeeper. He looks after 5000 acres of woods and farmland where he is rearing pheasants for a private shoot.

A big part of this land is owned and farmed by Philippe Grilhe, a former French clay pigeon shooting champion. The rest is owned by other local farmers. The latter allow them to use the land for shooting in return for Stephan shooting rabbits and the occasional deer who eat their chickens and damage their vines. He tears around the fields on a quad bike when he returns from work surveying his terrain, checking his decoys and traps.

Stephan and Philippe have reared hundreds of pheasant chicks which they gradually release into the woods. They have also installed several feeders filled with grain and water for the young birds in and around the woods. Despite this, Stephan says, many of the young birds are inclined to fly off to pastures new.

My owners suggested to Stephan that the chicks should be put into feeding pens with plenty of food so that the foxes can't get at them. This is what they do on pheasant shoots in England which encourages the birds to stay put when they are old enough to fly.

In France organised pheasant shoots, where the birds are driven by a dozen or more beaters, are rare. Normally "Le Chasse" (shooting) is open to anyone with a gun licence. The French "chasseurs" can access large areas and they have a habit of shooting almost any bird or animal that moves; sparrows, starlings, crows, pigeons, etc. The season starts in October and ends in February. At the end of the season they often abandon their poor hunting dogs who are left to fend for themselves. Some of them are picked up by the RSPCA but others end up being run over by cars or simply die of hunger.

Stephan and Philippe go to Spain in December to shoot driven partridge and pheasant. Last year they went to the Sologne region near Tours in the Loire department to shoot duck. Stephan is a good shot. We stalked a Roe deer on our local farmer's land, in fields not far from our house. Stephan shot it with a .22 rifle at a range of about 100 metres. After he had skinned and gutted the beast Stephan gave me a few cuts of meat called venison to eat. It was quite rich but delicious.

Other than Vicky, our French neighbour's bitch, I had two other friends who I used to visit and play with regularly. One was an elderly Lhasa Apso called Oscar who belongs to April and Freddie, and the other is a bitch mongrel terrier called Foxy who is owned by David and Diana.

Oscar told me he thinks he's about 14. He's a wise old thing with a very calming influence on me. After all, his breed originated in Tibet and these dogs guarded the Buddhist monasteries. Although I have never been there I am told Lhasa Apso is the name of the capital of Tibet. Oscar had long grey and white hair and a lovely curved bushy tail. He didn't see too well but he liked my company and he tolerated me chasing him around Avril's garden. Sometimes Oscar gave me the odd nip if I got too boisterous. When we go for walks, sadly, he can't keep up but instead he sits watching me running in and out of the vines. Lhasa Apsos are renowned for their acute hearing. If I got lost he would bark and guide me back to base. Even if he couldn't see me he could hear me. Oscar was quite happy for me to finish up his food while we both sat under the dining-table when Avril and Freddie were entertaining.

Foxy, who is so called because he looks like a fox, is much younger than Oscar. He is only three and behaves like a puppy. I race around with him and he jumps on my back biting my ears and tail when I let him. Occasionally when I have had enough I pin him to the ground, bare my sharp teeth and give a low menacing growl. David and Diana adore Foxy and they take him everywhere, even to restaurants. He adores them. They have a great game when they howl at each other with Foxy emitting a high pitched wailing sound.

David and Diana live near Eymet where half the population is British. They have been living in the area for thirty years, and before they built their new house they owned a lovely château near Castillonnes. They also have a house in the hills near Malaga in southern Spain, and two years ago they found Foxy sleeping in a dustbin in their local village.

It is not the first time they have rescued dogs. When Diana was living at the château she took in dogs she found wandering about on her land. Apparently these hunting dogs were often abandoned by local chasseurs after the shooting season when they decided they were surplus to requirements.. But, unlike Foxy who is much smaller, Diana was unable to adopt these strays but instead took them to the Croix Bleu in Bergerac.

Eymet has several bars and David frequents all of them. His favourite however is Le Café' de Paris whose Patron, Jean Michel, is a great friend. They have known each other for thirty years. I am allowed in this bar provided I sit quietly and don't grab the customers by the trouser legs when they pass - a bad habit of mine I am told. My favourite bar is the PMU the French equivalent of a betting shop where people can put money on horses. PMU stands for Paris Mutual. The reason I like this bar is because I meet the owner's dog called Toby. He is a Griffon Basset Vendee.

He is a sweet dog and is always pleased to see me. He has scruffy hair, a bit like a poodle but he has a bigger head, more like a wolfhound. He has lovely eyes and he is very kind and gentle. We play in the café for hours while my owner sits drinking beer and studying the racing form. Toby is much bigger than me and usually manages to pin me down on the floor, but he's very gentle and will release me when he realises I have had enough of struggling to get out of his grip. The PMU is owned by an English lady called B and her French husband, Pascal.

Eymet is a strange place. It is a small bastide town with 2000 English people living there - half the population. I meet lots of English dogs including all types of terrier - West Highland Terriers, Norfolk Terriers, Yorkshire Terriers and Jack Russells

The town has its own cricket team and an English shop selling everything from baked beans to PG Tips tea . On market days there is a van selling fish and chips. You can find all sorts of English fare at the market - everything from locally brewed English draft beer to pork pies, Cornish pasties, pork sausages and bacon. On another stall there are hundreds of second-hand English paperbacks for sale.

The strange thing about Eymet is that the English and the French all seem to get on very well, as do us dogs.

COYPU

Coypu were introduced from South America to Europe by fur ranchers. They are large, herbivorous semi-aquatic rodents. They have coarse, dark brown outer fur with soft under fur and webbed hind feet which helps them swim quite fast. The Coypu can be mistaken for a small beaver but beavers' tails are flat and paddle-like as opposed to having round rat-like tales. Because of their destructive feeding and burrowing behaviour they are regarded as pests. They feed on river plants and destroy river banks and the sides of lakes.

BERTIE
SEES EVERYTHING
SHOOTING UP

Taking a walk on a refreshingly cool June evening after the previous days' temperatures had been in the 40s it was interesting to observe the variety of crops shooting up all around us. In a large field directly opposite the house a new crop of sunflowers has sprung up with their heads turned towards the sun. An avenue of prune trees adjoining will soon be producing ripe, sweet plums. Walking up a hill past the Château Paradis vines, on which small green grapes are appearing, we came to a recently harvested cornfield.

A small wood borders this field from which a young roe deer shot out and stopped for a heartbeat in the middle of the field. I had a clear site of it and gave chase. I sprang off my lead like a missile. Despite my brave chase, the deer disappeared into a field of sunflowers. I was bidden back by my owner and we continued our walk.

Above me I noticed a huge bird of prey hovering - a buzzard with a massive wingspan. I kept a low profile, sticking close to my owner's heels. For I thought this creature would be swift enough and strong enough to swoop down and carry me off.

I often see a smaller bird of prey - a Peregrine Falcon I believe - perching on overhead telephone wires. He's smaller but faster than a buzzard but he appears not to be interested in me. Instead, he sits waiting to dive on smaller animals like rabbits and field mice - easy prey for his supper.

We arrived at a lake which was being put to use for irrigation. Alain, our neighbouring farmer, had left a tractor running with its revolving back axle turning a pump. A submerged pipe, joined to an oil drum floating on the lake, was linked to a network of other pipes which snaked from the banks of the lake to a large field of maize.

Water was being pumped from the lake and being sprayed intermittently in a high, wide arc over the maize. The maize (like corn on the cob) was already well above head height and is used for feeding livestock.

We returned through a wheat field, yet to be harvested, and down a line of prune trees past a second, fuller lake which evidently had not yet been used for irrigation and back through the vines. The château and its 16 hectares of vines are for sale. The owner had been asking in the region of 1m Euros but now she has dropped her price to 800,000 Euros. My owners have sampled some of the 2004 red and thought it was excellent. They say that the 2009, which can be found in some local supermarkets, is not so good.

Back at the house, the garden is coming along. The roses that were planted last year are thriving, as is the lavender. My owners have planted five hibiscus bushes and potted seven hydrangeas in enormous terracotta pots. The bamboo plants they put in along the west boundary of the courtyard are shooting up nicely. A wisteria, planted against the south facing wall of what were the pigsties is doing wonderfully and has climbed to a height of 3 metres. The two grass areas we seeded last year are a bit like a curate's egg - i.e. good in parts. They have needed constant water sprinkling and certain patches have had to be re-seeded.

We have two fruit trees, one producing wild cherries and the other wild plums which are too bitter to eat or cook but will be ideal for chutney. The two tall marronnier (chestnut) trees and the one plane tree in the courtyard were lopped in May and are looking healthier, letting in more light and allowing a better view of the pretty, stone cottages which border the east side of the courtyard.

The local "arboriste", Alain Benn, did the job of pruning them. Their leaves had been falling on the tiled roofs of our "dependences". They had been clogging up the gutters of an adjoining cottage and a row of stables. The taller of the two chestnut trees is over 30 metres (100 feet) but Alain was up in the top branches with his chainsaw as quick as a squirrel.

Tied round his waist were a series of ropes and tackle on a harness similar to that of a mountaineer. He showed me a special knot he tied, designed by an Austrian climber, called a Prusik which enabled him to winch himself twenty feet up into the branches of the chestnut tree without having to scale the trunk itself.

He used a led weight like a plumb line to throw a safety rope over branches above him. I was terrified he might fall and I sat under the trees barking for him to come back down to earth. He kept shouting to tell me not to worry and to get out of the way of falling branches. He was more worried about my safety than about his own.

I am enjoying these long lazy summer evenings watching the garden mature and bloom, listening to the chirping cicadas and the birds singing in the trees while trying to trap the odd darting lizard in my paws. There are wonderful sunsets making the sky a deep red. When I smell burning barbecue coals mixed with a few sprigs of lavender I know I'm in with the chance of a Toulouse sausage.

BERTIE MEETS A GULF WAR VETERAN

Just outside Bergerac, on the road to Bordeaux, is a little hotel with a big bar and shaded veranda called Chez Jakmy. We sometimes stop there for a coffee on the way to shop in Leclerc because I like to play with the resident spaniel. His name is Coco and he is from Brittany. They call his breed un 'Espanole Bretagne'. In English that's a Brittany spaniel.

It was there last year that we met David, a former British army officer who is partially blind after suffering post-traumatic stress following a tour of duty in Iraq. He was hardly able to identify where exactly on his table the patronne had placed his glass of wine. He spoke with a stammer and he was unsteady on his feet.

I sat beside him and he seemed to like that. He stroked me and spoke to me gently. He gave me the remains of his hamburger. I liked that, so instead of chasing Coco round the bar, I remained quietly at David's side - after all there's always a chance of more tit-bits.

David's story is very sad. After being invalided out of the army he has been unable to find a job, his wife has left him, he has had to sell their house near Chelmsford in Essex and he is being cared for by his parents who live in the Dordogne near Bergerac. When his mother and father go on shopping trips to Bergerac they leave him with the friendly patronne at Chez Jakmy and her few regular customers.

When we last saw David he told my owners that, so far, eye specialists both here in France and in the UK have been unable to do much to help restore his sight. He said he had been advised to rest and that his French specialist was hopeful that his eyesight would slowly return. The loss of sight, he was told, was due to his nervous disorder and time would be the healer.

David told us he had received little help from the army in finding future employment and he had been offered no counselling. He was expected to survive on a meagre Captain's pension. His plight reminded my owners of a TV documentary called The Wounded Platoon. It told the story of a group of American infantrymen when they returned home from Iraq. There were drugs, drink, suicides, wife beatings and murders. They were terrified, paranoid, damaged boys.

When we called into the Jakmy several months later my owners asked after David. The patronne told them he had gone to England for a few days to visit relatives. Sadly, she told us there had been no change in his condition and he still couldn't find his glass of wine without her help.

My owners recently came up with the idea of making their house in the Dordogne available to our brave soldiers injured in the war against the Taliban in Afghanistan, especially those suffering from post-traumatic stress. They are doing this through 'Give Us Time'*, a scheme to persuade owners of holiday homes both in Britain and abroad to allow members of our armed forces who have been invalided out of Afghanistan to have a quiet, comfortable place to rest and recuperate from their injuries.

The house here near Bergerac is ideal for this purpose. It is on one level so it will be suitable for wheel chair users, it is situated in a peaceful hamlet surrounded by Bergerac vineyards and there is a small supermarket in the nearest village only 2 kilometres away.

We have all sorts of ideas about how to help our boys recover from the trauma of war. For those who are mobile enough they could help the local wine growers with the vendange (the grape harvest in September). For others, with the full use of their legs, they could walk part of the pilgrim's route to Santiago de Compostella which traverses nearby fields. The way is clearly marked and the path winds past and below sloping vineyards. It would take about two months to walk all the way to Santiago de Compostella from this spot - something my owner is threatening to do with me in tow.

For those veterans who wish to learn or refresh their building skills there are two derelict cottages adjoining our house which are in need of renovation. The more seriously injured can sit quietly in the garden in the shade of two large Chestnut trees, they can swim in a neighbours pool or take a boat on a gentle cruise down the Dordogne river. My owner is a keen amateur landscape artist and he plans to arrange painting classes and expeditions for those with an artistic leaning.

Should any of the visiting veterans wish to let off their pent-up frustrations and emotions of war by firing a weapon again then our neighbour Stephan, who is the game keeper for a private shoot, will be happy to organise clay pigeon shooting sessions. He could also instruct them in the art of stalking deer, trapping coypu or shooting palombes. The latter which look like pigeons, are difficult to shoot because they fly very high. The local chasseurs rig up hides at the top of tall trees and set up decoys to attract them. These birds migrate from Scandinavia to Spain and Africa in early autumn and their path is almost directly over us here in the Dordogne.

31

I suggested to my owners that they should also consider offering rest and recreation to dogs that have been traumatised by war. There is a charity called Nowzad Dogs, dedicated to looking after strays who have been caught up in the Afghan conflict. We shall see what can be done, but any dog that has been brought back to Britain from Afghanistan will need a valid passport with proof of all the required vaccinations including rabies.

My owners read to me an interesting passage from Edward Stourton's book, 'Diary of a Dog-Walker'. He quotes from a pamphlet by Louise Clark, 'Animals at War', which records an impressive list of individual acts of canine courage and devotion.

At the outbreak of the First World War in 1914 a terrier called Prince managed to find its way from Hammersmith to the French town of Armentieres, where it joined its master on the Front line. During the Blitz bombing of London in the Second World War there was a spaniel who was trained to sniff out people buried alive beneath rubble. She apparently located more than twenty people, including two small girls who were dug out after the dog repeatedly returned to an area that rescue workers had already searched. Louis Clark's pamphlet also reports the shocking use of dogs as suicide bombers.

Edward writes that in modern warfare dogs have more usually been used as guards, messengers or rescue workers. He particularly enjoyed, as I did, the story of the dogs that went into action with the stretcher bearers of the Airborne Division during the Second World War. They came down on their own parachutes and were then ordered to quarter the ground in much the same manner that a Spaniel hunts through rough cover, looking for injured paratroopers.

My owners' godson, Alexander has recently returned from fighting the Taliban in Afghanistan as an infantryman with the King's Royal Hussars in Helmand province. He told us that sniffer dogs**, usually Spaniels or Labradors, were invaluable for detecting improvised explosive devices (IEDs) - mines hidden in the ground or in buildings.

The army regards these dogs as a battle-winning tool in the counter insurgency fight. I was pleased to hear that if one of these dogs is injured on patrol they are treated in the same way as any other injured soldier and will be evacuated from the battlefield by helicopter.

The local nationals usually keep Kabula fighting dogs which are a sort of mastiff breed used predominantly for dog fighting or baiting. They also keep them to maintain security in their compounds and as a means of raising the alarm. Alexander told us that sometimes the local dogs would attack the patrol but would usually be warned off with a well placed stone.

GIVE US TIME

* In 2011 the former Defence Secretary, Dr Liam Fox launched a partnership with Afghan Heroes calling on second-home owners to donate time at their properties to soldiers who have suffered from the trauma of fighting in Afghanistan. This initiative follows in the wake of the Help for Heroes charity which has helped to fund state-of-the-art facilities at rehabilitation centres in the U.K. such as Hedley Court. Called Give Us Time, the scheme enables property owners to donate time in their second home, holiday home or time-share property to returned soldiers recovering from the trauma of war. The logistics of the programme are managed by Afghan Heroes, which was founded in 2009 to support soldiers on the front line and families affected by military operations. The idea of the scheme is to help those who have suffered loss or injury to recover and to readjust to a normal civilian life.

** On Friday October 25th 2013 the Sun newspaper reported that two military dogs were killed in Afghanistan by the Taliban this year. An Arms and Explosives Search dog called Ric was on an SAS operation when he was cut down by Taliban bullets in August. Scout, a Labrador, was blown up by an enemy IED in January while leading a column of troops who all survived. The Sun reported that ten Army dogs have been killed in action since 2007. One of the others was a Springer Spaniel cross called Theo. He died from a seizure triggered by the death of his handler, L/Cpl Liam Tasker who was shot by a snipers in March 2011. Theo was awarded the posthumous Dicken medal, the canine equivalent of the VC. The deaths, the newspaper said, were a stark reminder of the huge sacrifice that Britain asks of its faithful hounds.

BERTIE
GOES
MOUSING

Whenever we go to the large garden centre, Desmartis, on the outskirts of Bergerac I am taken to see the pets. There are several glass cages containing hamsters, mice, rats, ferrets, chinchillas and rabbits near the exit to the main area outside selling plants, ornamental and garden furniture at the back of the building. There are also pens for pigs and chickens before you get to the plants.

This is a big treat for me and my nose remains glued to the glass, mesmerised by these creatures. I have to be dragged squealing from the pet area when we need to get on with the business of buying plants.

There is no doubt that these visits to the garden centre have sharpened my interest in rodents because last night I managed to catch my first mouse in our kitchen. I know that there are mice around because, snuffling around cracks in the floorboards of the rooms in the house, I can smell them. There are no foundations under the floors, and I can hear mice moving around freely under the floorboards which are laid on wooden joists resting on an earth floor base.

I have had one or two unfortunate experiences when chasing and catching other creatures in the garden and the field opposite our house. One hot summer evening I found a hedgehog, and had a rude awakening when I stuck my teeth into it.

There was blood everywhere but the blood wasn't coming from the hedgehog: it was coming from my mouth and nose. The hedgehog had curled up into a prickly ball and so I got a bunch of its spikes embedded in my mouth and nose.

Another time I pounced on a frog which sprayed me with a vile injection of its foamy poison. I came out of the long grass foaming at the mouth spitting out this sickly stuff. My owner had to wash my mouth out with water.

Let me return to the more enjoyable pastime of mousing.

Last year we had a wasp nest in the chimney and my owners lit a fire to get rid of them. They banked up the fire with wooden cartons and kindling to get a good blaze going. This did the trick but we got more than we bargained for. Down came the burning wasps, but with them came flaming mice.

I had been watching intently from the sidelines, dived into the fireplace and locked on to one of these burning mice, smoke pouring from my mouth.

I had to be restrained while the remaining dead mice and wasps were shovelled into the dustbin. Not to be put off by this experience, I continued to search for mice but I didn't manage a clean kill.

Then one day my owners detected a mouse crawling under a cast iron radiator in the kitchen. They moved the dresser standing in front of the radiator and I squeezed behind and somehow got my nose under the radiator. I remained glued to the spot for what seemed like hours.

I could clearly smell a mouse hiding behind the radiator. It really was a cat and mouse situation. Or should I say, "softly softly catchy-monkey"

Finally the mouse ran out from its hiding place and I pounced. I locked my teeth round its neck and shook it the way I shake my toys before tossing them around the room. I must have broken its neck because it appeared motionless and it was no longer squeaking. I proudly carried it in my mouth to show my owners who pronounced it quite dead.

BERTIE
GOES DOWN
WITH
TICK FEVER

On All Saints Day I went down with dreaded tick fever, a particularly virulent killer found in south-west France. I went from being an active, happy chap to being almost totally immobilised. I was being sick, refusing to eat and, when helped to my feet, was very wobbly.

Almost everything in France is closed on All Saints Day (Tous Saints). When my owners called our vet near Bergerac there was an emergency vet's number left on their answer phone. They called the emergency number but there was another message. They needed to act quickly so they tried another vet in the Dordogne directory. The vet was in Eymet. This time they struck lucky. There was a clear message saying in French and English that their emergency vet was on duty in Miramont just across the departmental border in the Lot-et-Garonne.

It was 11.30 am and they had to move fast to get me there before the vet shut up shop for lunch dead on 12pm. His name was Dr Costes, a no nonsense, serious type - a farmers' vet with a good reputation. He took from his cabinet a long, thin wire tube and without a word of warning threaded it up through my penis. Surprisingly I hardly noticed this deft move. It wasn't very painful and I hardly uttered a whimper. Mind you I was half comatose from the infection by this time.

The last time I felt so poorly was when I picked up some sort of virus in Finsbury Park in London where all sorts of scruffy, fierce dogs roam. I must have picked it up from one of them. The South African vet who treated me was pretty casual and didn't give me a correct diagnosis.

Instead he guessed that it might have been some sort of tick, which turned out not to be the case, and administered a dose of Avantix. This is a very strong anti-tick drug which I reacted to badly. I got very low and was fading fast. To make matters worse he suggested I have a course of strong antibiotics. They made me feel so bad that I had to be taken in overnight at the veterinary surgery. They put me on a saline drip and I had to spend two nights shut up on my own in a small room at the back of the surgery. The whole episode was a nightmare both for me and my owners who had to fork out £1400 for my treatment. We haven't been back to this particular veterinary clinic since.

Having extracted the tube, Dr. Costes was able to take a urine sample which immediately confirmed that his diagnosis was correct. He said that I had contracted an infection called Biosopris* from a tick particular to the Aquitaine region of France and prevalent in autumn. This attacks the kidneys and he put me on a course of diuretics to clean them out.

No sooner had I got home than the telephone rang. It was our friends, Avril and Freddie calling from England. They said they were on their way to Heathrow to get a flight back to France because Oscar, their Tibetan terrier, a Lhasa Apso and my good friend, had died the previous night from a heart attack.

They asked if my owners could meet them at Bordeaux airport that same evening? Well this was difficult because Lyndia would have had to stay with me in the house without any means of transport to get me to the vet urgently should I suffer a further relapse. What could my owners do? They could hardly refuse to help out with poor little Oscar having died that very morning. So my principle owner went to meet them at Bordeaux with very little time to spare.

He later told me he had to negotiate thick traffic on the Bordeaux périphérique in the pouring rain. He could hardly make out the road signs he told me. Somehow he managed to get to Bordeaux airport on time and entered the arrivals hall just as Avril and Freddie emerged from passport control.

"My poor baba Oscar. They've killed my baba Oscar. They should have called me before putting him down," Avril exclaimed as she was greeted by my owner.

Avril's hired help, Diana, who had been minding Oscar, had apparently taken Oscar to the vet in the middle of the night. He said there was nothing he could do and recommended that Oscar should be put to sleep. The vet turned out to be none other than Dr. Costes and the decision had been taken there and then in the early hours of same morning that I was taken to see him.

Avril drowned her sorrows with a large vodka at the airport bar. In the car driving back she calmed down and confirmed that Dr. Costes was, in fact, a wonderful vet and that perhaps he had made the correct decision. After all, she admitted, Oscar was 15 years old, was stone deaf and hadn't been in the best of health,

"But my poor baba. They could have at least called me. I shouldn't have left him. Perhaps he wouldn't have died if I hadn't left him," she cried.

The next day we attended Oscar's funeral service at Avril's former home in Puysserampion near Miramont. She had spent twenty years restoring and converting a couple of tobacco drying barns into a beautiful five-bedroomed house complete with swimming pool and landscaped gardens. Then two years ago she sold it to a Swiss banker.

They buried Oscar in the shade of an avenue of Cypress trees. It was a beautiful, sunlit November day and the assembled few drank a glass of Armagnac as a final toast to this sweet little dog. I hope that God will guard over him in the same way that he was bred to guard the Buddhist temples in Tibet.

TICK FEVER

* Tick fever, (also known as Babesiosis or Piroplasmosis), is one of the main tick-borne diseases of south-west France. It can be life-threatening and can lead to complications such as kidney failure. Early signs of infection are high fever with shivering and trembling, complete lack of energy and food and water refusal. The urine turns brown, and the gums are paler, due to breakdown of red cells. If diagnosed, the dog is treated with an injection that kills the parasite, sometimes in combination with antibiotics. There are several ways of protecting a dog from ticks: anti-tick treatment applied to the skin, an anti tick collar, checking the dog for ticks regularly, as well as vaccination.

BERTIE REPORTS AN ENGLISH MURDER

When my owners go to buy wine 'en vrac' (from the barrel) they visit a lovely little local Bergerac château called Maine Chevalier just off the Plaisance to Eymet road. It is hardly a chateau but instead a large barn with an office where wine can be tasted before purchase. You have the option to bring your own 5- or 10-litre container which is filled from 1000-litre vats or simply buy the wine in 5-litre boxes.

The wine growers own a very friendly Brittany Spaniel who plays with me amongst the vines while my owners go off to taste last year's crop of wines. They are never disappointed and the they usually come back with a couple of 5-litre boxes of Bergerac rouge which has cost them the princely sum of 22 Euros.

Opposite the turning to Maine Chevalier, on the other side of the Eymet road, there are signs to a golf course. The owner of the golf course, an Englishman called Peter Fuller, was apparently running short of money and hoped to recoup some of his losses by selling

English roast lunches to British ex-pats, more than two thousand of whom live in Eymet, a small bastide town about 10 kilometres from his house.

Well, not long after we arrived in the area we heard from our friendly French neighbour, Bernard, that the owner of the golf course had been murdered by another Englishman, a builder who had been working for him.

Bernard speaks good English because at one time he had been a teacher in the United States. He always speaks to me in English and, unlike most French people, he pats me when he sees me and gives me biscuits.

There was certainly no mistaking what apparently had been a gruesome and bloody murder. Sure enough the crime was reported the next day on the front pages of the local regional daily, Sud Ouest*. Bernard translated the story and read it to me in English.

Peter Fuller, aged 67, had died on Saturday night or early Sunday morning, and his body was discovered by his ex-wife on Sunday at midday. He had suffered head wounds which were thought to be caused by a blunt instrument.

Fuller lived alone in a large house near Plaisance but for the last three weeks he had a young Englishman lodging with him who is said to be in his 30s. When the gendarmes arrived at the scene the man had disappeared. The Sud Ouest reported that the man, who has not been named but who was the prime suspect in the murder case, boarded a plane at Bordeaux airport bound for London where he was detained by the British police.

Two of Fuller's cars were missing. One, which had broken down or been involved in an accident, had been found abandoned near Fuller's house. The other had apparently been used by the assailant to get to Bordeaux.

On July 1st 2009 the Sud Ouest reported that the suspected assailant of the retired English entrepreneur, Peter Fuller was Neil Andrew Ludlam, aged 30. He could be sent back to France on the recommendation of English magistrates under "un mandat d'arrêt européen".

The body of Fuller was found by his ex-wife the next morning at what was described as a "scène d'horreur". He had been hit several times over the head with a blunt instrument. According to French police Fuller was found face down in a sea of blood - "une mare de sang". There was evidence of a fierce fight. Furniture was turned upside down in the living room, the kitchen and in the dining room near the bar where empty bottles of alcohol and glasses were found. There were traces of blood on the walls and on the furniture.

Ludlam, who had been staying with Fuller, is reported to have fled the scene in one of Fuller's cars. He was arrested by the British police at Luton airport when the aircraft he boarded in Bordeaux landed. He is reported to have had a large sum of cash on him.

One of the other unsolved mysteries is reported to be the theft of two cars stolen from Wheeler's house. One was a red AX Citroen found crashed 12 kilometres from the scene of the crime. The other was a Mercedes coupé which has not yet been traced. The police have not been able to confirm whether this was the car Ludlam used to drive to Bordeaux airport.

It is also not known whether anyone else was involved in Peter Fuller's murder. However the Sud Ouest reported that this affair had created a degree of turmoil - "emoi" - in the British community living in the Dordogne.

Ludlam languished in a French jail for three years until he was finally found guilty of murdering his expatriate employer. He was sentenced by the Périgueux Tribunal de Justice to 18 years in prison for stabbing and battering to death Peter Fuller in a drunken attack.

The court heard that Mr. Fuller, 67, a retired Total oil engineer, was found face down in a pool of blood with cracked ribs, 59 injuries and seven stab wounds, including a punctured lung.

*THE SUD OUEST NEWSPAPER

The Sud Ouest is the regional daily newspaper for south-west France with separate editions for different departmentes. On June 30th 2009 the Sud Ouest broke the story of the horrific murder of Peter Fuller, a retired Englishman who was bludgeoned to death by another Englishman who had been working for him.

The Daily Telegraph carried the story of the trial on Saturday June 2nd 2012. Ludlam is reported to have received well below the maximum 30-year term for murder after Charles Charollais, the prosecuting judge in Périgueux, argued that he had shown remorse and accepted responsibility for his crime.

BERTIE
& THE CHINESE
WINE BUYERS

L iving amongst the Bergerac vines we thought it was time to discover some of the better known and more expensive Bordeaux wines. The Bordeaux tourist office organises all sorts of different visits to many of the 10,000 châteaux in the area.

The great thing was that they didn't mind me coming along for the ride. My owners plumbed for a morning tour of two châteaux near St Emilion - Le Vieux Maillet which produces the renowned Pomerol and Château Ferrand which produces a fine St Emilion Grand Cru.

Before embarking on this guided tour we decided to stay close to Bordeaux at Libourne in a small hotel called L' Hotel de France. They were happy to let me stay in the same room as my owners. A former coaching inn, the hotel had a certain old world charm but our room, which gave onto a busy road, was small, dank and uncomfortable. There wasn't much space for me to sleep on the floor so I slept on the bed.

In the reception area I noticed a group of Chinese sitting at a low table littered with half empty wine bottles. To my surprise, when my owner asked them whether they had found some good wine, they asked him whether he would like to taste the wines they had chosen to market back in China. They all made a great fuss of me which was a surprise because I thought they ate dogs in China. But one of them even sat me on his lap and stroked me. They gave me some nuts they had been eating in between their wine tasting. They were a bit mad. My owner made signs to me that they were drunk.

Their guide and interpreter was a Chinese lady called Fanny Antoine who had a commercial wine business in Libourne.

"Please come and sit with us and try our wines. Taste this one first. It's a 2004 Château Grangère Grand Cru St Emilion," she said.

My owner explained that he was no expert but just an ignorant tourist. Tentatively he took a sip.

"What do you think?" asked Fanny refilling his glass.

He said it was the best red wine he had ever tasted.

"Smooth, full bodied, slightly sharp but, by the same token, rounded and mellow."

"Yes. Very good. I agree," she said.

"Good , yes, you like? Have some more," the Chinese buyers* chimed in unison.

This was becoming a bit embarrassing as we had nothing to offer in return. My owner resorted to congratulating them on finding such a good wine, asking whether they were exporting this to China.

"You want to know what price we paid for this Château Grangère?"

asked one.

"The price is 15 Euros a bottle. But you wouldn't pay that in the shops. I did a deal with the château because my clients bought several thousand bottles. They have bought two crates for shipment to China." said Fanny

"How much wine do you get in two crates?" asked my owner.

"Thirty six thousand bottles," she said

The cargo would be divided into approximately a third Grand Cru St Emilion, a third Pomorol and a third Grand Cru Pauillac. The Château Grangère St Emilion was expected to be sold in China for the equivalent of £40 a bottle, the Pomorol 2005 purchased for 19 Euros a bottle, for £60 and the 2009 Pauillac for in excess of £100 a bottle

"What about the rumour that the Chinese mix this expensive wine with coke?" asked my owner.

"Yes, that was before our people became more educated about wine. They liked to mix their wines with Sprite lemonade. That's because the Chinese have a sweet tooth," said one of the buyers.

The Chinese buyers left early for Paris the next morning, a little worse for wear, and we set out for the Bordeaux Tourist Office to join our tour.

CHINESE WINE BUYERS

French winemakers in the past have been shocked at tales of Beijing's nouveau riche mixing Coke with vintage Bordeaux, but their sales growth relies on the Chinese market.
Wine bars where sophisticated young Chinese sip claret and fine white wines

are now common in Chinese cities and the Asian nation is already the world's biggest importer of Bordeaux. Chinese drinkers knocked back 48 million bottles of the stuff last year. Overall, France shipped $660 billion worth of wine to China last year, more than two-thirds of all European wine sales there. The trade in wine with China is vital for the survival of producers in the Bordeaux region.

The Times (Monday June 17 2013) ran an alarming story about a young Chinese woman studying wine-making in France being hit in the face with a champagne bottle. It had been thrown at her by a Frenchman shouting racist abuse. The attack was condemned as xenophobia by the French Interior Minister, Manuel Valls. Chinese investors buying up struggling vineyards in France are resented. Apparently the culprit was one of three men who were drunk and who insulted six Chinese students at La Tour Blanche School of Viticulture and Oenology near Bordeaux.

BERTIE
THE
BULLFIGHTER

I had an interesting experience when we stopped off in the Camargue on our way back to the south-west from the Cote d'Azur We had been staying at a friend's house at Grimaud, a village in the hills above St Tropez. I had a lovely relaxing time there sitting by the pool in the shade of some tall cypress trees, playing with a neighbour's poodle and occasionally diving into the water to cool off.

The fun started when we decided to stop off at Saintes-Marie-de-la-Mer, the capital of the Camargue, a huge area of marshland near the mouth of the river Rhone. As we drove south of Montpellier we passed ranches and riding stables with white Camargue ponies tethered. Other horses were simply running around wild in the marshlands, some grazing, others trotting through pools of water. The Camargue is also famous for its fighting bulls reared there. These bulls end up in the bull rings of the bigger towns in the region like Arles, Nîmes and Beziers.

I love chasing and running with horses so my adrenalin was at full throttle when we reached Ste Marie. I was taken for a stroll on the beach and I waded into the sea to cool off. This helped me to get the sight of all those horses out of my system.

We stopped for lunch in a small restaurant and Le Plat du Jour, was Toro (Bull). The humans ordered two Bull steaks and they gave me a slice to chomp on - it was delicious. After lunch my owners took me further into the centre of town looking for shops selling authentic Camargue clothes such as moleskin trousers and patterned shirts worn by gardians - the men charged with rearing the bulls and rounding them up on horseback.

Suddenly I was aware of a very strong smell - something intense and bestial quite different from that of my equine friends. I strained hard at my lead trying to pull away from the main street towards the town square. My owners became aware that there was something going on. At first they said they thought that it might be some sort of demonstration or festival.

They allowed me to pull them towards the noise, while all the time the smell became quite mesmerising. As they turned out of a small street into the square they realized what was going on. Immediately in front of us was a circle of white-washed walls and tiers of seats rising high above. There were hundreds of people inside, cheering and whistling. It was a bullring and the smell was coming from the bulls inside, high on testosterone.

The bullfight* turned out to be for Novellas - for younger bulls than those used in normal bullfights. These young bulls don't get killed but, instead, amateur bullfighters, dressed in white trousers and shirts and wearing plimsolls, show off their bravery and skills with their capes.

They try to get as close as possible to the charging bull sometimes even giving it a slap or a kick. If these wannabe bullfighters get into trouble they simply leap back to safety over the wooden guard fence. We were all keen to get inside to see the bulls but the place was packed. As we squeezed in amongst those standing my owners lifted me onto their shoulders for a better view. This became awkward for others trying to see so we tried to get closer. By this time I was frantic to get close to the action. There must be bull-baiting** instincts bred into us terriers, though this cruel sport became illegal in Britain two centuries ago.

A spectator gestured for us to go forward and, while my owners were threading through the crowd, I slipped my lead. I ran full pelt down the steps of the gangway, leapt over the wooden safety walls surrounding the ring and gave immediate chase to a young bull who had just entered the arena.

This was fantastic fun. The animal was snorting and pawing at the sand with its hooves. I was barking like fury, high on adrenalin. As I approached the bull charged me and tried to hook me with his horns, but I skipped out of his way just in time. Clearly the bull was incensed with my presence and he started to chase me round the ring, snorting fire as he came closer.

The crowd had gone mad and were shouting: "Olé Olé", each time the bull charged past me, I swerved and feinted to avoid him like a true matador. As I turned to acknowledge the applause I found myself flying through the air. I landed in a heap, quite dazed and winded. The bull had caught me unawares and had tossed me half way across the arena. For some miraculous reason his horns hadn't pierced me but had gone either side of my body. Instead I received an almighty head-butt. It was a stunning blow like being hit by a train.

As he prepared to charge again, four brave, aspiring matadors jumped into the arena, swirling their capes, distracting the bull from his deadly pursuit. The next thing I knew I was bundled up in one of these capes, chucked over the barrier and caught by an official. When he found my owners we were immediately thrown out of the arena, severely reprimanded and told how lucky I was to have survived.

*BULLFIGHTING

Although Spain is the home of bullfighting France also stages different types of bullfights. These take place close to the Camargue in cities like Nîmes, Arles and Beziers. With bullfighting being banned in Catalonia, Spanish style bull-fights, where the bull is killed, have become more popular in France. However in the smaller arenas there are different variations of the sport where the bull is not killed but is only used by young aspiring matadors to learn their skills in the bullring. These fights are known as Novellas or Capellas. Bullfighting in the Provence and Languedoc areas is known alternately as "course libre" or "course camarguaise".

This is a bloodless spectacle in which the objective is to snatch a rosette from the head of a young bull. The participants begin training in their early teens against young bulls from the Camargue region of Provence before graduat-ing to regular contests held principally in Arles and Nîmes, but also in other Provençal and Languedoc towns and villages. Before the course, an encier-ro—a "running" of the bulls in the streets—takes place, in which young men compete to outrun the charging bulls. Afterwards, the bulls are herded back to their pen by gardians (Camarguaise cowboys) in a bandido, amidst a great deal of ceremony. The stars of these spectacles are the bulls, who get top billing and stand to gain fame and statues in their honour, and lucrative product endorsement contracts.

**THE HISTORY OF BULL BAITING

In England during the time of Queen Anne, bull-baiting was practised in London at Hockley-in-the-Hole, twice a week. This cruel sport was also reasonably common in provincial towns. At Stamford and at Tutbury, a bull was tied to an iron stake so that it could move within a radius of about 30 feet. The object of the sport was for the dogs to immobilise the bull. Before the event started, the bull's nose was blown full of pepper to enrage the animal be-fore the baiting. The bull was often placed in a hole in the ground. A variant of bull-baiting was "pinning the bull", where specially-trained dogs would set upon the bull one at a time, a successful attack resulting in the dog fastening his teeth strongly in the bull's snout. The bulldog was bred especially for this sport. The practice of bull baiting was finally outlawed when parliament passed the Cruelty to Animals Act of 1835, which forbade the keeping of any house, pit, or other place for baiting or fighting any bull, bear, dog, or other animal.

BERTIE

FLIES TO

ALDERNEY

In August I set out from the Dordogne with my owner for Alderney* - a tiny island just off the north-west coast of France. Once owned by France, Alderney, which is one of the Channel Islands, has its own parliament and its own laws - smoking is still allowed in the pubs. My owners had decided to get married there and Lyndia was to meet us there, flying in from Southampton. You can get married in Alderney in 4 days, much quicker than in England.

The temperatures had reached 40° centigrade as our little Peugeot joined the Angoulême périphérique. It was midday, and the traffic was at its height as the French were all going home for lunch. I was fast expiring in the searing heat and was panting feverishly despite the car windows being open. My master was desperately looking for a petrol station to stop for water; it took what felt like hours before he could find an exit where a service station was signed.

As soon as he found one he filled up a bucket with water and threw it over me. As we drove further north and beyond Nantes, mercifully the weather broke and it began to rain. We arrived at St Malo where it was still raining and refreshingly cool. I remember we found a little bistro down a side street in the old town where my owner ordered 'moules frites' and he threw me some mussels to munch. I cracked open the shells with my sharp teeth and they were delicious.

I had become expensive extra baggage. It was because of me that we had to take the ferry to Guernsey from St Malo instead of crossing by the weekly ferry from the port of Dielette near Cherbourg, direct to Alderney. It is only 8 miles and would have taken little more than an hour at a minimal cost. However we were informed that they didn't take pets or cars, only foot passengers. Alderney, we were told, wasn't a port of entry for pets and that, instead, we would have to go through Guernsey and then fly to Alderney.

Sadly, my owner had to pay 200 Euros to sail to Guernsey, then stay overnight before taking the Aurigny flight to Alderney. This was another expense they hadn't originally budgeted for. The cost for the three of us - I had my own seat - on a tiny, twin prop Islander, was £300 one way.

We touched down on the grass landing strip and entered the wooden hut that served as the arrivals lounge. It seemed as if the clocks had gone back 50 years. We could have walked to St Anne's, the capital, in 10 minutes. Instead we jumped onto an ancient double decker bus that served as the only public transport. It dropped us in the main street a short distance from our B&B.

I had a wonderful time exploring the island and its beaches and moreover, I met several other Border Terriers one of whom, a bitch called Molly was owned by a lady who lived on the island called, Nicky. I met her two dogs every morning in the local café in the main street. At first we didn't know her name. A few days later, by a stroke of coincidence, we saw Molly looking lost at an evening open-air pop concert. Another lady we met said: "That's Molly, Nicky's dog."

The name must have registered in my owner's brain because when he eventually found her in the crowd he asked her whether she was the same Nicky that knew his brother. She was delighted to hear he and Lyndia were getting married. She agreed to be their witness at Alderney's only registry office, the next day. She turned out to be a marvellous host and entertained us at her lovely house on a hill overlooking the port. She tied coloured bows round the necks of us dogs for the wedding ceremony and drove us to the town hall in her battered old car draped with flowers and coloured streamers.

My owners didn't know anybody else on the island to ask to their wedding except for a married couple from Essex, John and Sandra, who also owned a male Border Terrier. They had left him back in England to be looked after by a friend while they were on holiday. When we saw them in the same café on the high street they made a great fuss of me putting me on their lap and feeding me biscuits and sausages.

They were invited to the registry office but John didn't seem a bit interested in the bride and groom. He gave them little recognition and while muttering his congratulations he was, all the time anxiously looking for me. When I followed my happy owners out of the town hall there was John, all smiles, welcoming me with open arms. Picking me up he said:

"Oh good, there you are Bertie. I thought I would find you here. Hello Bertie. Good boy Bertie."

It was all my owners could do to stop him running off with me.

The other Border Terrier I met on the island was my arch rival in the agility class of the Alderney dog show, which I took part in the next day. It turned out that this dog had won the same event the year before and clearly knew the ropes. He dashed round the course but got the last obstacle down. I followed, three dogs later, and my only problem was getting through a dark tunnel which my owner persuaded me to

71

crawl back down after I tried to turn round inside it and escape back into the light. We made up time after I cleared all the other obstacles

Hooray! I won and I have a rosette and a silver cup to prove it.

*ALDERNEY

Alderney is the most northerly of the Channel Islands. It chose independence from France back in 1204 when it declared its loyalty to the Duke of Normandy. Over the following years Alderney retained its own entity, not having much to do with the rest of the world. However, this changed in the 19th century when the British came to fortify the island. A harbour was built on which to deter incoming attacks from the French. There was an influx of both English and Irish labourers leading to rapid anglicisation of Alderney at this time.

During the Second World War the island was occupied by German forces. Nearly all of the islanders living there at the time fled before the Germans arrived. The Germans surrendered the island in May 1945 and it wasn't until December of the same year that islanders began to return.

The 20th century was a time of great change for Alderney. In the late 1930's the island's airport was built and it has gone from generating most of its income from agriculture and turned to tourism and finance. Unfortunately the last speaker of the Alderney language, called Auregnais, passed away in the 20th century. It was a language thought to be a dialect from Norman times.

BERTIE
MISSES
THE BOAT

We returned to the Dordogne by the same circuitous route and all was well until, two months later, my owners decided to return to England in October, on the ferry from the Spanish port of Santander.

This made things particularly complicated. Some of this was self-induced as I my owners totally misjudged distance and the time it would take us to get from Bergerac to Santander. They had been told it would take 5 hours but we hadn't even reached the Spanish border in that time. So you can guess, we missed the boat!

This meant we had to wait for the next boat - to Plymouth instead of Portsmouth - four days later! At yet further expense, I had to have my inoculations and my passport* stamped for entry back into the UK all over again.

Lyndia had a pressing business engagement, and had to fly back to London from Bilbao the next day. So we were left to our own devices.

For some reason the Spanish don't seem to like dogs staying in hotels. After my owner tried several in town he resorted to having to rent a small apartment for two nights so I didn't have to sleep in the car.

We had already been to our vet in France the morning we left for Spain, but my vaccination and inspection have to be carried out 24 hours before I leave French or Spanish soil, not within 24 hours and not after 48 hours. This meant a second visit to a vet, this time in Spain. The vet, who we visited at a small fishing port near Bilbao called Castro, thought I could travel within 24 hours and stamped his passport accordingly.

Once at the port the following day, with only an hour to spare, we were informed that my passport was incorrectly stamped. We had to run to the nearest vet in Santander. There was a queue of several other frantic ex-pats whose passports were also incorrectly stamped. Another 30 Euros was required and a phone call to my previous vet, who confirmed that I had been inspected at 10am the previous day and not 7pm - the actual time he had entered in my passport. The problem was sorted with half an hour to spare before the ferry left for England. The Spanish vet in Santander must have been making a packet out of all these misguided British pet owners whose passports had been incorrectly stamped!

The crossing itself was quite an ordeal. I had to stay almost the entire 48-hour voyage in a small, metal cage along with about fifty other barking and yelping dogs in adjoining cages. There was no light and just a metal bowl for water attached to the inside of the cage door. I didn't get any sleep and neither did my owner, who kept coming to check on me and to let me out for a stroll around the deck. We were both exhausted when we got to Plymouth, and my owner had a hangover having drunk far too much in the bar to get over the shock of nearly missing the boat. God, we were pleased to be back on home turf!

PASSPORTS FOR PETS

The passport for pets scheme has made it possible for thousands of British people and their pets to be able to travel to France and to other European countries without having to put their animals into six months quarantine when they return home. Bertie was therefore able to travel with his owners to France.

Britain is one of the few countries in Europe, which is rabies free, and so it continues to have strict quarantine laws. Before the Passport for Pets Bill was passed in the early 90s, your animal, usually a dog or a cat,was required to be left in kennels when returning to Britain for six months.

Now it is much easier and the animal's passport simply has to be updated 24 hours before embarking on a ferry or a plane for the UK. Previously the same animal was required to travel after 24 hours and within a 48 hour period after that. The time limit for travel has been increased to a period of five days after, but not before, 24 hours from the time the passport has been updated

The most important vaccination is the one against rabies. Bertie was required to wait six months after his rabies jab had been tested positive before he could return to England. Interestingly the Department for the Environment Food and Rural Affairs (DEFRA) refers specifically to dogs, cats and ferrets no less, and this is how it describes the Passport for Pets Scheme: otherwise known as (PETS), was introduced so that pets entering or returning to the UK would not need to undergo the usual compulsory 6-months quarantine period to protect against rabies.

Any dog, cat or ferret coming from a country that does not qualify under PETS will have to undergo the compulsory 6 months quarantine on arrival. To bring your dog, cat or ferret into the UK under the Pets Passport Scheme, you must follow the following procedure, in strict order: Have your pet micro-chipped so that it can be properly identified.

Have your pet vaccinated against rabies by a certified veterinarian. (Your pet must be given a rabies vaccination AFTER it has been micro chipped there is no exemption to this rule, even if it had a current rabies vaccination before being micro chipped. A blood sample from your pet must be tested by a certified veterinarian and shown to provide a satisfactory level of protection against rabies.

Following the satisfactory test result and the veterinarian issuing the PETS documentation, you must wait 6 calendar months from the date of the blood sample before you can enter the UK. Your pet must be treated for ticks and tapeworms by a certified veterinarian not less than 24 hours and not more than 5 days before it is checked in with an approved transport company for travel to the UK.

The cost of getting your animal a passport, the vaccinations and the micro chipping is about £500. Then each time you bring the animal back into the U.K., you are required to take it to a vet for ticks and tapeworm vaccinations and have the passport stamped to verify this had been done. This costs between 50-60 Euros. If you take a ferry crossing, even though your animal must stay in the car, there will be a surcharge of approximately £30 for each pet. Therefore, anybody wishing to come in and out of Britain with more than just one animal should do his or her sums carefully before buying a second home in France or in another EEC country.

BERTIE
WALKS FOR
NEPAL

We had just got back to London from France when we heard about a charity dog walk in Regents Park. The event was taking place the day after we returned. I was tired and emotional after a long drive through France and a rough ferry crossing from Calais to Dover.

The Day of the Dog charity walk was in aid of the Kathmandu Contemporary Arts Centre. It was held to celebrate Nepalese Dog Veneration Day. Established in 2007 to promote local artists' work, abroad, the centre was completed in 2010 and stands in the gardens of the Royal Museum in the capital, Nepal. It offers studio space and scholarships to emerging Nepalese artists. The Day of the Dog charity walk is the brainchild of a lady called Celia Washington. She is an, artist herself, and had the idea to help struggling Nepalese artists when she visited Nepal in 2008.

A bit of eastern Karma, my masters thought, would be just the sort of tonic I needed. I was clearly out of sorts from three days of travelling and not a bit pleased to be back in the big smoke.

Before reporting to Celia and paying a nominal entry fee for the walk, my owners decided it might be a good idea to let me have a run around in the park so that I could meet and play with a few dogs. Later I would have to be kept on the lead when I joined the other dogs - all of whom seemed to be on their best behaviour - taking part in the charity walk

In the distance I spied a liver brown Labrador happily playing with a Spaniel. I was straining on the lead to go over and join them so my master let me go. I was about 20 yards from the other two dogs when, out of nowhere, came a Chihuahua running towards me from another direction, his owner in pursuit. I would say they were at right-angles to the course I was on.

Spying the fluffy white dog out of the corner of my eye, I immediately turned sharp right and flew towards him like an Exocet missile. Within seconds I had the Chihuahuas furry body in my jaws. Unable to immediately separate the two of us, my master picked me up with the Chihuahua still hanging from my locked jaw. After being cuffed about the head several times I finally let go, and the poor, stunned Chihuahua fell to the ground in a heap yelping at his owners feet.

The expletives started to fly and my master could only say in a mild mannered way:

"I'm so so sorry. This is quite unlike my Border Terrier. He's normally such a sweetie and loves all dogs and humans."

"Put that bloody dog on a lead. He's a liability. I've a good mind to report you to the park constable," came the reply.

Undaunted, my master walked over to the Chihuahua, patted him and checked for any injuries or whether I had drawn blood. Fortunately he appeared to have a clean bill of health.

In an effort to placate the owner as well as his dog my owner, in his best bedside manner, said:

"Oh don't worry. He seems to be quite alright. What a sweet little dog."

"Fuck off and take your horrible terrier with you," came the sharp retort.

Beating a speedy retreat my owner, looking, over his shoulder, shouted:

"I am terribly sorry, it won't happen again."

I'm afraid I have been involved in a number of other unfortunate altercations which have been an embarrassment to my owner.

There was the time when I pounced on a male Jack Russell being led by a young girl. I hadn't gone for his throat or anything but just got a hold of his fur. His owner became hysterical, and the next thing I knew I was being prodded by an old man with a stick so I let go of the dog.

My owner was furious with the man and called him a wanker - an ignorant townie who knew nothing about terriers wanting a scrap. It turned out that the old boy was the girl's father. My owner had to apologise profusely for his offensive remarks, which he said were, made in the heat of the moment.

On another occasion I got a little bit more than I bargained for when a Staffordshire Bull Terrier suddenly went for me. His walker had told my owner that he was normally friendly, but she also had in her charge a bitch mongrel Labradoodle (a cross between a Poodle and a Labrador).

Obviously the dog was trying to protect the bitch. That wasn't my concern and I gave as good I got and we both locked jaws on each other's necks. By this stage the Staff's owner had become hysterical and was trying to pull her dog off me. My owner told her to calm down and tried to talk me into letting go. Finally, after several minutes, he pulled my tail so hard that I let go.

Another time I was chasing a hoodie on a bike until I couldn't keep up any more. We had turned round and continued our walk when, out of nowhere, the same guy sped past on his bike punching my owner's head. Try as we might we couldn't catch him.

Returning to Regents Park and the Kathmandu Charity walk, not to be deterred by the Chihuahua incident, we joined the marchers and dogs taking part. Before we set off, the organisers, dabbed a tikka - a little red dab of powder - on my forehead and hung a garland of flowers round my neck.

The assembled company included 40 dogs and 78 humans. There were all sorts of dogs. There was a poodle called Sherpa Tenzing, two Wolfhounds called Archie and Fergus, a Jack Russell bitch called Dolly, a Pug called Rocco, a Cairn called Panda and a pack of King Charles Cavaliers and their protector, a Labrador called Max.

We all started to stroll round Regents Park moving at a slow and sedate pace. I soon became bored with this slow procession and I become restless pulling on my lead. There was a gorgeous, curly haired Labradoodle bitch up at the front of the procession which I was keen to get up close and personal to. I guessed that she was on heat.

Worried that I would cause another diplomatic incident, my owners decided it would be best to cut away and make our excuses to Celia.

When we found her and said goodbye I was mildly surprised that she invited me back to take part in another of her charity dog walks which she organises annually in a different London park each year.

Since starting these charity events Celia has raised a total of £150,000. This money not only goes towards providing grants for Nepalese artists but also helps fund an animal treatment centre in Kathmandu.

BERTIE MEETS AN URBAN FOX

I would like to tell you about my breeding and why chasing foxes is in my blood. We Border Terriers originate from the rough, bleak, hill country on both sides of the border between England and Scotland. This is sometimes known as 'The Border Country'.

The breed was developed by the farmers and shepherds of the area who used terriers to help contain the local fox population. Foxes in The Border Country are a predatory animal of particular concern to sheep farmers whose flocks wander relatively free over many thousands of hectares of heath and heather-covered land. In the 19th century, when fox-hunting developed into the sport we know today, the breed began to be used as part of the more formal fox-hunting scene.

The Border Terrier's job is to 'bolt' foxes when they 'go to ground'. In other words when foxhounds and the field (horse-riders) in pursuit of the fox stop because the fox has gone into one of its underground lairs, the Border Terrier has to go underground and either 'bolt' (chase out) the fox or stay with it and bark. This is to indicate to those above ground where the fox is located so that they can dig down to their quarry. The Border should not be too forward in attacking the fox underground. Rather he should threaten him and preferably chase him out.

Almost all of the requirements listed in the Official Breed Standard, (The Breeder's Bible) , are specifically chosen to make the breed able to do the job of work for which it has been designed. For example the Border terrier should be "Capable of following a horse, combining activity with gameness." The breed should be built for endurance and a certain amount of speed - but not for sprinting or excessive speed.

A Border Terrier should be able to go to ground and follow a fox into any space into which it can go. The foxes found in Border Country are not large and can get into fairly small spaces. Borders have to be able to do likewise. Yet another aspect of the breed is that though it has to be 'game' underground, it should not be aggressive with other dogs, which sadly is one of my failings when I meet other entire dogs who show their own aggression. A trouble making Border that has to integrate with a pack of hounds would not last very long before the hounds put him in his place - or worse!

On my nocturnal walks in the back streets of Finsbury Park, near where I live in London, it is amazing the amount of urban foxes that emerge from almost nowhere. They are attracted from the wild open spaces to the easier hunting grounds of suburban London. Here there is plenty of food to scavenge for. All sorts of goodies are thrown out by the wasteful humans who buy too much for their own needs because of cheap deals offered by supermarkets. Bits of chicken, half eaten hamburgers, fish and chips leftovers and meat bones are all there for the picking, in dustbins, plastic waste bags and even on the pavements. These urban foxes consequently appear very healthy, robust and quite tame.

90

With hunting foxes in my genes, I go crazy chasing these brush tailed creatures through back gardens, over walls, in the park at the back of my house and in the local school playground. Somehow, however hard I chase them, they outwit and outrun me, slinking off like shadows in the night.

Then, one cold winter evening, I came across a big red dog fox*, with a brush as long as his streaky white body, who jumped over a garden wall in the street where I live. He simply stood there on the pavement looking at me. He didn't bat an eyelid at my furious barking, He just sat there silently watching me. My owner who, when he's had a bit to drink and feels so inclined, sometimes lets me give chase. This time he kept me firmly on the lead and the fox walked past us on the other side of the road.

A few nights later we saw what must have been the same fox, and once again he stood his ground ignoring my frantic barking.

The third time we saw him my owner let me go and still the fox stood his ground. We stood there looking at each other. I was barking my head off and he was looking at me with his bright, yellow, hypnotic eyes as if asking:

"What's all the fuss about?"

We gave him a name. We called him Francis after the patron saint of animals, St Francis of Assisi.

Well, a few weeks later my owner was walking me in the same park behind our house. He usually lets me off the lead here because there is an oval grassed area the size of a cricket pitch which is railed off. He knows I will normally just run around in the centre chasing a ball he throws for me.

On this occasion, however, I spied a white Pomeranian bitch on heat the other side of the railings. Somehow I managed to squeeze through the rails and as the Pomeranian turned the corner and trotted out of the park I gave chase. For some reason the bitch and her owner were nowhere to be seen, and I ran up and down the adjoining streets ignoring the calls from my owner and somehow dodging the passing traffic.

After ten minutes I was completely lost and exhausted. I had lost the scent of the Pomeranian and I had lost the scent of my owner. I could just hear his faint cries calling out my name, but I had no idea of his whereabouts. I wasn't sure how to find my way out of the maze of side streets I had gone down.

As I walked slowly towards the distant calls of my owner I suddenly became aware of my bushy tailed friend, Francis, at the end of the street. As I got close he turned his head, as if beckoning me to follow him, and walked slowly in the opposite direction. Exhausted, I followed in his footsteps and finally, after turning several corners with the fox still a few yards in front, there we were in the street where I live.

Francis had found me and led me home. So don't be surprised if one evening you happen to witness the strange sight of a Border Terrier being led by his owner round the dimly lit back streets of Finsbury Park with a Fox walking by their side.

*URBAN FOXES

The red fox has become a familiar sight in London since arriving from the English countryside, where it has traditionally been shot as vermin or chased by hunters and packs of hounds. With upwards of 10,000 foxes now roaming the capital, urban living clearly suits them. Foxes first sought refuge here after World War II. Since then they have swapped wild rabbits and farm chickens for a diet of discarded takeaway food and other garbage.

These urban foxes are noticeably bolder than their country cousins, sharing side walks with pedestrians and raising cubs in people's backyards.

Foxes have even sneaked into the Houses of Parliament, where one was found asleep on a filing cabinet. Another broke into the grounds of Buckingham Palace, reportedly killing some of Queen Elizabeth II's prized pink flamingos. Generally, however, foxes and city folk appear to get along. A survey in 2001 by the London-based Mammal Society found that 80 percent of Londoners liked having the animals around. Some residents even deliberately attract foxes by putting out food for them to eat. However, other Londoners say foxes are pests that dig up lawns, scatter garbage, terrify pets, and leave behind a foul scent.

EPILOGUE

B ertie's adventures in this book of short stories are largely in south-west France in the region of AQUITAINE. Eight hundred years ago, back in the 12th century, Aquitaine was ruled from Bordeaux by the English King, Henry II who married Queen Eleanor of Aquitaine. Their fiefdom extended from the Pyrenees in the south to the Loire in the north and Toulouse to the south east.

It was one of the richest domains in medieval Europe. The historian, Alison Weir has written one of the finest biographies of Eleanor of Aquitaine and I quote some passages from her book:

"Prologue: 18th May 1152

"In the Romanesque cathedral of Poitiers a man and a woman stood before the high altar exchanging wedding vows......

"..... few would have guessed, from the lack of pomp and splendour, that the marriage of this couple was to change the face of Europe.

Yet the bridegroom was Henry, later called Plantagenet, Count of Anjou and Duke of Normandy. Not only did he hold strategically important domains in what is now France but he was also the heir to his mother Matilda's claim to the Kingdom of England.

".......Henry was about to extend his territories even further, by marriage to one of greatest heiresses of the Middle Ages. The woman who stood beside him was Eleanor, Duchess of Aquitaine, the Countess of Poitou and former Queen of France. Not only did she own most of the land between the Loire and the Pyrenees, but she was also renowned for her loveliness...."

Weir describes Aquitaine, as "opulent" and "sweet as nectar" thanks to its vineyards dotted about with forests, overflowing with fruit of every kind and endowed with a superabundance of pasture land. Wealthy thanks to its lucrative export trade in wine and salt, the English attained great influence in Bordeaux because of the wine trade..

Now the English have returned to Aquitaine. There are English estate agents in most of the local market towns, supermarket shelves display baked beans, steak and kidney pies and PG Tips. Fish and chips are sold in many of the pubs and Sky satellite dishes beam in English TV channels to thousands of homes. There are English libraries, cinemas showing English films, English book shops and English wine growers

In one small market town called Eymet half the 5000 population is English. It has a cricket club, an English food shop, bars selling pints of Guinness and a Farrow & Ball paint shop. At Pau in the Gers there is even a pack of English bred foxhounds with an English master of foxhounds. There are more British living in Aquitaine now than ever. They are a new breed, a product of the social change in Britain during the 1960s and 1970s – people who come to France because property is cheaper, social services are better, the climate is warmer and the countryside is less spoilt.

Avon Priestley is a former correspondent for the BBC and the Independent. He's been working on a house near Bordeaux surrounded by vineyards which he bought in 2009. The Amazing Adventures of Bertie the Border Terrier is taken from a blog he has been writing, while renovating the property with his wife Lyndia

Avon is 65. Bertie is 5.

Avon is writing a second, longer book – An Englishman in the Dordogne. This is an insight into living in a part of Aquitaine known as "Little England" and in the French department the British ex-pats call "Dordogneshire".